Christmas Revelation

A Candle Star Christmas Production

by
Shell Isenhoff

ISBN-13: 978-1477425954
ISBN-10: 1477425950

Candle Star Press
www.michelleisenhoff.com

A Note to Directors:

Thank you for choosing to use a Candle Star Christmas Production in your church or school. My purpose in writing each play was to create a pageant that even small groups could produce simply. (They have all been produced in my own church of 200 people.) But stronger still was my desire to immerse viewers in a powerful story that left no question about the true meaning of Christmas. Christ's coming to dwell with man is only part of a whole gospel message, which is clearly presented in each script. My hope is that this play will help you spread that message in your community this holiday season.

Merry Christmas and break a leg! And to Jesus Christ be all the glory.

Shell Isenhoff

Find additional
Candle Star Christmas Productions
on my website:

www.michelleisenhoff.com

Table of Contents

Summary

Accompanying his sheep to overnight pasture, a father tells the story of their people to his son. The events he narrates are mimed on stage, illustrating God's plan leading up to the Deliverer. As they settle down to sleep, Mary and Joseph arrive at the inn in the background. The spiritual battle told in Revelation is represented during the birth, and Satan is defeated as Joseph holds the new baby aloft. Angels awaken the shepherds, who rush to the manger.

Length

Candle Star Christmas Productions are designed to run between 45 minutes to an hour when music is included at scene breaks.

Cast of Characters

Speaking Characters:

God (in white)
Jacob the shepherd boy
Josiah's father - large narrative part
Mary
Joseph
Angel (singer of final song)

Nonspeaking parts:

2 sleeping shepherd uncles (optional)
Satan (in black)
Adam
Eve
Abraham
Isaac
Moses
King David
Two brothers (civil war) and a
Foreign captor to lead them off
Inn keeper

Stage Setup

The stage is split between the shepherds in a field, who need only props on the floor, and a stable setting. It would be helpful to have a low partition (hay bales or a choir loft half-wall?) to shield Mary when she's giving birth in scene three, with plenty of room behind for God and Satan to move. Also maintain room for the miming that takes place in scene two.

Prop List

Campfire
Blankets (shepherd bed rolls)
Knife (Abraham and Isaac)
Crown (King David)
Manger
Doll or a swaddle of blankets to represent baby Jesus
Shepherd staffs (optional)
Fruit (Adam and Eve)

Music Recommendations

At the end of most scenes, an option break for music is inserted. This is left wide open on purpose, because the organizations that produce this play will have vastly different musical talents available. They may even choose to skip some or all of these opportunities. However, music offers a great distraction while switching scenes, and it provides a whole additional platform for worship. Here is a list of suggestions to fill these opportunities:

Songs sung by children's Sunday school classes or school classrooms

Vocal solos or groups performed by children or adults

Instrumental solos performed by school children or adults

Brief piano interludes

Traditional carols provide simple, recognizable tunes for instrumentals. Vocal arrangements might consist of carols as well, or be drawn from the variety of contemporary music available.

Mary, Did You Know? written by Mark Lowry and Buddy Greene, is available commercially sung by a variety of artists. A "canned" version may be played over the sound system, or it can be performed live by members of your organization.

Similar treatment may be given *Gloria*, by Michael W. Smith, which is also widely available.

Christmas Revelation
by Shell Isenhoff

Scene One

Two shepherds are sitting around a fire. Two more are already sleeping (optional).

Father: (With a stretch and a yawn) So, Jacob, it is your first time taking the sheep to pasture overnight. How do you like it?

Jacob: I love it, Father! I'm big enough to do the work now, aren't I?

Father: (Affectionately rumpling hair) You're growing up way too fast. But we've had a busy day and it's time to rest. Under your blankets now.

Jacob: All right, but will you tell me a story first? Please?

Father: A story! Now?

Jacob: Yes. Tell me the story of our people.

Father: All right, one story. I'll tell you about Moses and how he led our people out of Egypt.

Jacob: No, start at the beginning, Father.

Father: But it is late! See? Your uncles are already snoring!

Jacob: I'm not tired. Not really. Please?

Father: (Sighing) All right. From the beginning.

Optional break for music.

Scene Two

Note: This scene is written to mimic the old-fashioned, oral story-telling tradition of pre-industrial cultures. Father can discreetly read the part while the appropriate characters enter and mime the narrative. God is active throughout, but at the appropriate places, Satan must struggle against Him, trying to derail His plan and stir up trouble.

Begin scene with shepherds still sitting or sleeping around fire. God and Satan present on stage. Adam and Even lying "dead" on their backs. Other mimes waiting in order of appearance just off stage. Manger is set up to one side for Mary and Joseph's entrance at the end of the scene.

Father: Many thousands of years ago, God created the beautiful world you see all around us. He made the starry sweep of heavens and the bottomless depths of the sea. And he made a garden and filled it with every good thing—shady trees and colorful bushes, crisp, sweet fruit, and flowers so fragrant you longed to bury your nose in them. He set within the garden gentle animals and birds of every song and color, and it was very good. But he saved his greatest creation for last.

Out of the dust of the earth he fashioned man and woman, and he placed them in the garden. He walked among them and talked with them, and he set them over every created thing. They were to care for the garden and the creatures within it. Only one kind of fruit he withheld from them.

But one day the serpent (*mimed by Satan*) came to the woman to deceive her. He bade her eat of the one fruit, and she did. And she gave it to the man. And sin entered the world.

The man and woman were removed from the garden, and life became difficult and painful. They endured hard toil and reaped little from their labor. Fear and viciousness entered the wild beasts. Greed, envy, malice, and death sundered their relationships, and God looked on them with pity.

God: (Speaking to Adam and Eve) You have disobeyed me and broken fellowship with the Lord, your God. But I will not hide my face from you forever. I will send a Deliverer who will reconcile you unto me once again.

Father: Many years passed and our father Abraham walked on earth. God led him to a new land and renewed his promise. Though Abraham was old, and his wife was past the age of childbearing, God chose to make him the father of many nations. Furthermore, God promised to bless the whole world through him. From his line the Deliverer would come.

In due time a son was born to Abraham, and Isaac grew to be a young man. But the day came when God tested Abraham. He called him to a far off mountain and commanded him to sacrifice his only son. Abraham obeyed, believing yet in God's promise.

Show Satan excited, thinking the Deliverer's line will be quickly broken as Abraham's sacrifice of Isaac is mimed. Next show him defeated.

God: Abraham, stop! Now I know you love me. Look behind you, there in the thicket. I have provided a ram to take the place of your son.

Father: Abraham's children multiplied and moved to Egypt where they became a nation so great and numerous that the Egyptians feared them and enslaved them for four hundred years. But God remembered his chosen ones. He raised up Moses and delivered his people from bondage with miraculous deeds and an outstretched hand. He settled them in a good land, flowing with milk and honey, and he called them back to himself when they strayed.

He raised up a king for them after his own heart. David loved the Lord and followed in his ways, and God renewed his promise to him. The Deliverer would come from David's own line, and his kingdom would never end.

But again and again our people rebelled against God. Israel was split apart, and brother fought against brother. And foreign nations conquered our land and carried our people away. But always God has remained faithful. Our people live still. Though the Deliverer has not yet come, the promise remains.

Jacob: (Yawning and stretching) Thank you, father. I hope someday I can tell our old stories to my children as well as you tell them to me.

Father   : I'm sure you could tell them now, as often as you ask for them. Off to bed with you now.

Jacob: Okay. (Snuggles under a blanket) Father, sometimes I wonder when the Deliverer will ever come.

Father   : (Also pulling up a blanket) So do I child. So do I.

In the meantime, being mimed on the other half of the stage, Mary and Joseph are being led to the stable by the innkeeper.

Optional break for music.

Scene Three

All shepherds are sleeping. Focus shifts to the stable.

Joseph: (Settling into a blanket) We've traveled far. I'm so tired I think I could sleep for a week!

Mary: (Shifting) I think I could too, if this baby would just let me find a comfortable position.

Joseph: (Raising up to look at her) Just think, Mary. The Son of God! You are carrying the Son of God! (Laying back and looking at the ceiling with his hands under his head, talking to himself while Mary starts to signal the onset of labor.) I never would have guess when I met you that you'd carry the Son of God. You're just an ordinary girl. I mean, I love you, of course, but I never would have picked you out of a crowd and said, "That's the one who will carry God's Son!" We're both just ordinary, you and I. Why on earth would God would choose us?

Mary: Joseph?

Joseph: Just think, out of all the millions and millions of people that have ever lived—or ever will live—he chose us. (Chuckles) Doesn't that just blow your mind? I mean, really? I still can't get over it.

Mary: Joseph, I think it's time.

Joseph: I wonder what it will be like to raise Him. The Son of God, I mean. Will he be different than other children? Will He be quiet or talkative or… (Suddenly stops talking) What did you say?

Mary: (Laughing) I think the baby's coming tonight. Help me up.

Suggested music for the birth scene, Mary Did You Know?

Note: This was originally performed in a church with a choir loft. The half-wall worked extremely well to shield the upcoming birth scene while the standing characters of God and Satan and Joseph were easily seen. You may have to get creative.

Mary and Joseph walk to a sheltered spot. Satan hovers around them greedily. God is there too. When Mary lies down (out of sight) to give birth, Joseph kneels with her. Satan and God begin the most exaggerated power struggle of the play. At the final "Great I AM" at the close of the song, Joseph stands up, holding the baby up toward heaven triumphantly. At the same time, Satan makes a final lunge but is driven back by God, each arm outstretched. God relaxes, therefore Satan sags too, but he keeps his arms stretched out, getting the idea for the cross. Make this clear by having him exaggerate the position, then go away cruelly pleased with his new strategy while God smiles at his Son in Joseph's arms.

Scene Four

Joseph, Mary and the baby are in stable in full view. Jacob wakes up and sees an angel (final singer), and starts tapping his father awake. Father moans and swats him away in his sleep. Jacob persists.

Father: (Exasperated) What! Jacob, what is it?

Jacob points, terrified. Father looks then falls back into his blankets.

Father: I *told* Miriam not to pack the spicy sausages.

Angel: Do not be afraid.

Father springs awake, terrified.

Angel: For, behold, I bring you good tidings of great joy, which shall be to all people. For unto you is born this day in the city of David a Savior, which is Christ the Lord. And this shall be a sign unto you; You shall find the babe wrapped in swaddling clothes, lying in a manger.

Angel sings just the chorus of what will be the final song accapella: "Gloria. Oh, Gloria in excelsis deo. Gloria. Oh, Gloria in excelsis deo. Alleluiah." *Then angels backs up into the background.*

Father: What in the name of Jehoshaphat's beard was that?

Jacob: (Excited) Father, don't you see? It's the end of the story! It's the Deliverer!

Father: No, it couldn't be!

Jacob: Yes! Didn't you hear what he said? A Savior! Come on!

Jacob drags Father, followed by optional shepherds, down an isle and around the congregation while final song begins, back to the stage, and approaches the manger where they bow.

Play or perform closing song, Gloria *by Michael W. Smith. Optional host of angel singers could join the original angel.*

At this point, you may wish to give your minister a few moments to address the audience and close the service.

MICHELLE ISENHOFF has written over a dozen novels for teens, tweens, and kids as old as 91. Her work has been reader-nominated for a Cybils Award, the Great Michigan Read, and the Maine Student Book Award. She also placed as a finalist in the Kindle Book Review Book Awards and the Wishing Shelf Book Awards. A former teacher and longtime homeschooler, Michelle has been lauded by the education community for the literary quality of her work, which is regularly purchased for classroom use. To keep the genres separate, her religious works are published under her nickname, Shell Isenhoff.

Find Michelle at **www.michelleisenhoff.com**.

Additional Candle Star Christmas Productions

Eyewitness Christmas

In a humorous blend of biblical and modern culture, an aspiring journalist named Luke is trying to break into the periodical, National Scroll, with a fantasy Christmas article, but editor Liebowitz rejects it, demanding facts and authenticity. In a second attempt, Luke conducts four interviews to learn exactly what happened that first Christmas night. What he discovers changes everything.

A Soldier's Christmas

In the Shenandoah Valley, in the midst of the American Civil War, the meaning of Christ's birth and death are given greater significance to one rebel soldier after his life is spared by a friend who gave up his own.

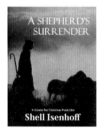

A Shepherd's Surrender

Three Bethlehem shepherds return from their annual delivery of sheep to the temple for Passover. Samuel doesn't believe the newly crucified Jesus was really the Messiah. His reasons date back to a very personal tragedy that accompanied his birth. A visit from the resurrected Savior, however, convinces him of the truth.

Born to Take My Place

After being freed from prison, Barabas takes upon himself the task of learning who it was that took his place on the felon's cross. His search leads him all the way back to the manger.

The Lights of Christmas

A Judean family celebrates Hanukkah during the dangerous days of the first Jewish revolt. Eli, the family patriarch and witness to the death and resurrection of his older brother Jesus, explains to his grandchildren how the festival points to Messiah, who was born not to free Jews from Rome but to free all men from sin.

In a very traditional take on the Christmas story, Mary's father struggles to believe his grandson is the Son of God.

Made in United States
North Haven, CT
20 September 2022

24337544R00015